Easy To Make And Use

HOLIDAY
&
SEASONAL
BULLETIN BOARDS

by
Imogene Forte

Incentive Publications, Inc.
Nashville, Tennessee

Edited by Jennifer Goodman
Illustrated by Mary Hamilton
Cover by Susan Eaddy

ISBN 0-86530-137-9

TABLE OF CONTENTS

PREFACE

Bring seasonal color and cheer to your classroom from September to June with this contemporary collection of Holiday & Seasonal bulletin boards and patterns. Designed with the busy teacher in mind, this book features over 65 easy-to-make-and-use bulletin boards complete with patterns, construction suggestions, activities, border patterns and to make the boards more versatile and flexible, additional captions and ideas.

Over 50 patterns have been included to make the construction of these boards easy and quick. Simply enlarge the patterns by using an opaque projector or by drawing them free hand. Don't stop there though. There are dozens of other uses for these delightful patterns. Some additional uses include:

Bookmarks	Gameboards	Flannelboard Figures
Bookplates	Collages	Paper Bag Puppets
Awards	Screen Painting	Necklaces
Stick Puppets	Stencil Painting	Finger Puppets
Puzzles	Placemats	Party Favors
Name Tags	Booklet Covers	Greeting Cards
Mobiles	Stand-Up Tray Favors	Backings for Student Art-
Invitations	Window or Door	work, Homework or
	Decorations or	Photographs
	Worksheet Decorations	

Remember, students love to be a part of creating classroom bulletin boards. Utilize their talents and abilities by letting them color in and cut out the patterns, put up backgrounds, cut out letters or design the board. With the combination of the creative touches unique to you and your students and the ideas, activities and patterns provided in this book, the seasons and holidays are sure to come alive in your classroom.

This Book Belongs To:

Trick or Treat

BORDER INSTRUCTIONS

Patterns for borders have been provided at the back of this book. Each pattern is labeled with the corresponding bulletin board(s). Follow the instructions below to make them.

1. Use construction paper (size 12" x 18") or tagboard strips.

2. Cut the paper into 5" x 18" strips. Cut as many strips as necessary to enclose the bulletin board.

3. Measure the width of the border pattern selected. Beginning at one end, fold the paper strip in an accordian fold so that the width of the paper is the same as the width of the border pattern.

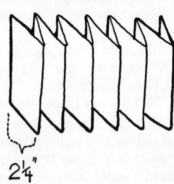

$2\frac{1}{4}$" $2\frac{1}{4}$"

4. Place a copy of the border pattern on top of the folded construction paper. Then cut out the border, leaving the folded edge uncut. DO NOT CUT ON THE DOTTED LINES.

5. The border will last longer if laminated. It may then be stored in large envelopes or rolled and stored in coffee cans when removed from the board.

6. Border patterns will also last longer when laminated. After lamination, cut the laminating film up to the edges of the pattern, leaving no extra film around the border. This will facilitate smooth tracing.

In addition to making borders, these patterns have been designed for use in other ways. The back of each pattern is a reproducible, solid outline. This side of the pattern may be reproduced to create name tags, student activity sheets, bookplates, awards, party favors, puppets and dozens of other things to add flavor and flair to daily classroom activities.

CONSTRUCTION AND USE

- Use real corn husks and real leaves if possible. If not, use the patterns provided and make them red, gold, brown, orange and yellow. Make the background black or gray, the grass green and the half moon yellow.
- Display student work on the board. This will be more meaningful if students are allowed to select their own best work to display.

ADDITIONAL BULLETIN BOARDS

A HARVEST OF GOOD BOOKS: Use the board to display new library books or have each student write the name of his or her favorite book and a few sentences about it on a pumpkin.

JACK-O'-LANTERN JAMBOREE: Give students a pumpkin pattern. Have them make and decorate a jack-o'-lantern and give it a name. Display on the board. Award prizes to the silliest jack-o'-lantern, the best dressed jack-o'-lantern, the scariest jack-o'-lantern and so on. To further extend the activity, have students write a story or poem about the jack-o'-lantern that they have made.

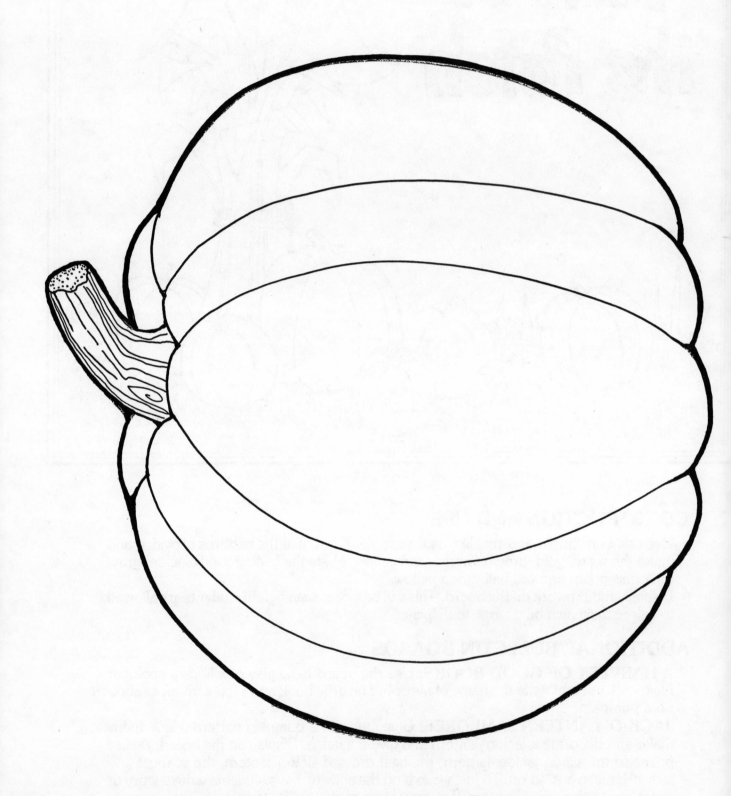

Half-moon pattern also makes a great name tag for open house, Thanksgiving or Halloween parties.

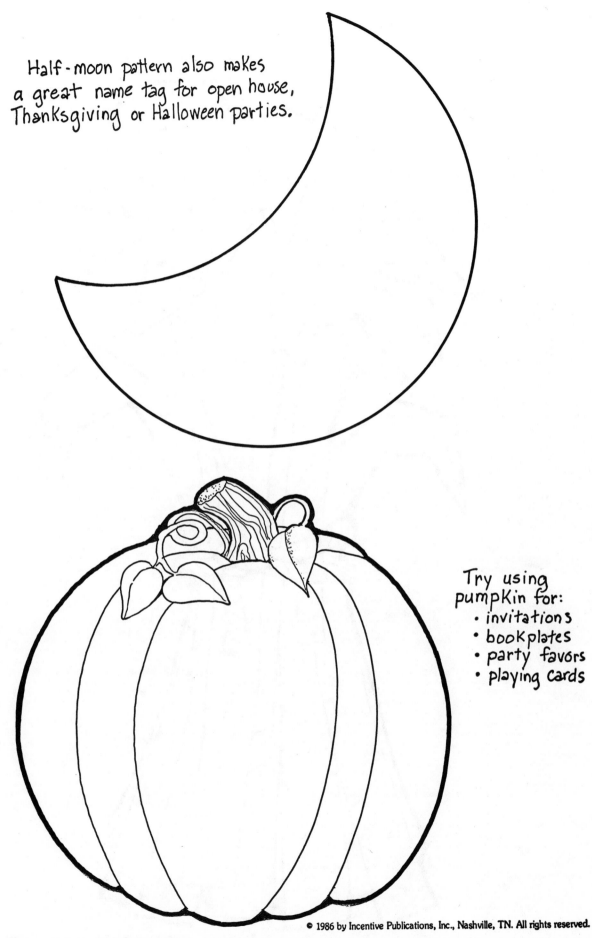

Try using pumpkin for:
- invitations
- bookplates
- party favors
- playing cards

COLUMBUS SAILED THE OCEAN BLUE IN FOURTEEN HUNDRED NINETY-TWO

CONSTRUCTION AND USE

- Make the water from two shades of blue paper or ask students to color it using chalk, crayons or tempera paint. Cut the ships from black or brown paper and the sails from white.
- Ask students to use reference books to find out more about the voyage of Columbus (or tell the story to younger children). Then have students write facts about the journey on sentence strips to be added to the board and label the ships with the correct names.

ADDITIONAL BULLETIN BOARDS

SET SAIL FOR GOOD CITIZENSHIP
SET SAIL FOR GOOD SPORTSMANSHIP
SAIL INTO FRIENDSHIP

Use any of the captions listed above. Reproduce a copy of the ship for each student. Ask students to list on the sail actions that they think will contribute to the desired trait. Display on the board.

CONSTRUCTION AND USE
- Reproduce a copy of the haunted house pattern for each student. Ask them to write a spooky story on the other side.
- Display the stories on the board.

ADDITIONAL BULLETIN BOARDS
WITCHES, CATS AND BATS ARE ON THE PROWL—HALLOWEEN IS NEAR: (Change near to here on Halloween day.) Use as a bulletin board for student work, book jackets or to announce a Halloween party, school carnival or open house.
BLACK CATS BRING BAD LUCK AND OTHER SUPERSTITIONS: Have students write papers about how and why certain superstitions got started.
YOU WOULD NEVER BELIEVE WHAT HAPPENED HERE ON HALLOWEEN NIGHT: Put this caption up on the day after Halloween. Ask students to write stories about what happened. Display the stories on the bulletin board.
OPEN HOUSE: Leave off the Halloween figures and use only the house to announce an open house.

Bat pattern can be enlarged to make a truly different Halloween mask.

You can use the cat pattern for party favors, invitations, puppets or greeting cards.

14

Enlarge pattern for door decoration, or have students cut out and color for use as a Trick-or-Treat bag decoration.

16

TURKEY TRIVIA

CONSTRUCTION AND USE

- Make the turkey out of brown construction paper using the pattern given.
- Provide each student with a brightly colored turkey feather. Ask them to write a trivia question on one side of the feather and the answer on the other. Pin several feathers on the turkey with the answer facing the board. Put the other feathers in a folder and pin to the board.
- Let students go to the board during free time to try to answer the questions.
- After all the students have had a chance, change the questions. (This can be used with different subjects such as social studies, math, geography, reading, music, etc.)

ADDITIONAL BULLETIN BOARDS

IF ONLY TURKEYS COULD TALK . . . : Have students write a story about a turkey. Display the stories on the bulletin board.

TURKEY TALK: Make a big turkey to be used for a hall bulletin board. Have students write thank-you's on the feathers to school workers such as the principal, cafeteria workers, secretaries, etc.

THESE TURKEYS WILL BRING MILES OF SMILES: Have students make turkey tray favors for a nursing home or hospital. Display on the board before distributing them.

Use as stand-up table decoration (see left), or as a door decoration.

CONSTRUCTION AND USE
- Cut big chunky letters for the caption from bright, autumn colored paper (brown, gold, rust or red) and the table from brown or rust. Cut the other figures from appropriately colored paper or from white paper and ask students to color in details with a felt tip pen.
- Use the bulletin board as a background to display student pictures or paragraphs describing what they have to be thankful for.

ADDITIONAL BULLETIN BOARDS
THANKSGIVING DELIGHTS: Have students write out and illustrate their favorite Thanksgiving recipes. Display them on the board around the large turkey. The recipes could later be compiled into a class recipe book to be presented as a holiday gift for parents.

PILGRIMS, INDIANS AND (teacher's name and grade) CELEBRATE THANKSGIVING: Ask students to draw and cut out their own pictures to add to the board.

AUTUMN TREASURES: Substitute the cornucopia for the food on the table. Ask students to collect autumn leaves, bunches of berries, seed pods, pine cones and other natural materials to display on the board.

Have students make finger or stick
puppets and put on a Thanksgiving play.

Patterns may also be used for name tags, or cut out and colored for greeting cards or booklet covers.

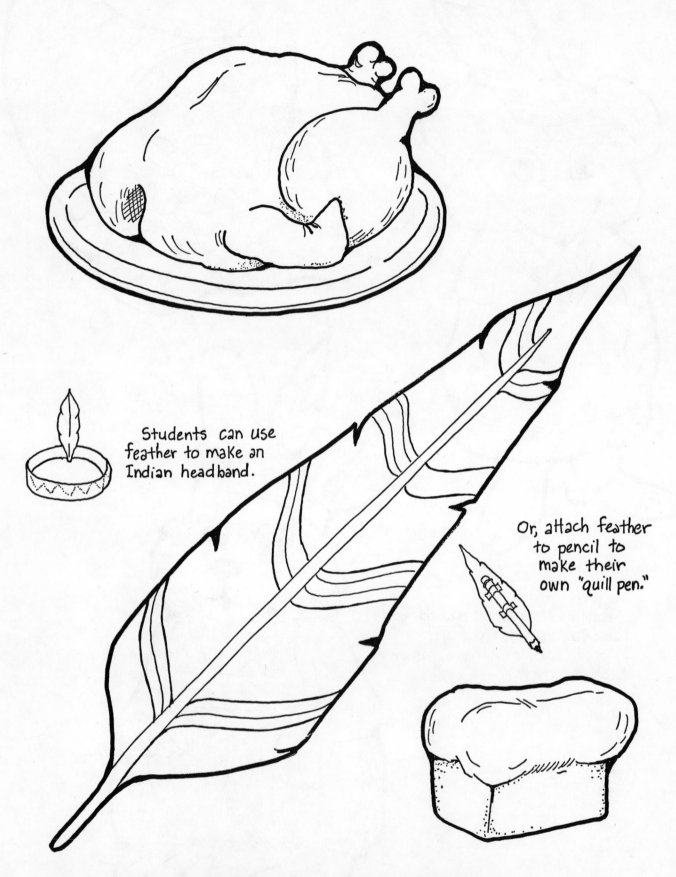

Students can use feather to make an Indian headband.

Or, attach feather to pencil to make their own "quill pen."

CONSTRUCTION AND USE

- Enlarge the snowman pattern and cut from a large sheet of white butcher paper. Make the hat and eyes from black paper, the nose from orange and the scarf from red. For a delightful change of pace, use real pieces of coal for eyes, a carrot for the nose, tree branches for arms and a real hat and muffler.
- Display book jackets with winter titles or plots around the snowman.

ADDITIONAL BULLETIN BOARDS

FROSTY THE SNOWMAN: Enlarge the snowman pattern and display on the board. Have students write stories or draw pictures to show what happened when the sun came out.

WINTER WONDERS: Have students do winter paintings for the board using dark blue paper, white tempera paint and silver glitter.

CONSTRUCTION AND USE

- Make the background out of dark blue construction paper, menorah from gold foil paper, candles from white paper and flames from yellow paper. Attach a folder to the board and label it Chanukah Wishes.
- Add a new candle on each day of the holiday. Ask students to work together to develop a Chanukah wish to be printed on the candle. (Candles should be added from right to left.)

ADDITIONAL BULLETIN BOARDS

FREEDOM FEELINGS: Print the following words on sentence strips to be displayed on the board around the menorah: joy, appreciation, belief, tradition, commitment, loyalty, happiness, devotion. Ask students to select one or more of the words to use as the theme of a paragraph expressing thoughts and feelings about religious freedom.

CHANUKAH HAPPENINGS: Ask students to research Chanukah symbols in reference books (dreidel, star of David, latkes, wrapped gifts, etc.) and draw pictures of how these symbols are used to celebrate Chanukah. Display the pictures on the board.

OH CHANUKAH - OH CHANUKAH - SING A SONG OF CHANUKAH: Add music notes cut from black paper to the board. Write the words to Chanukah songs on chart paper and display.

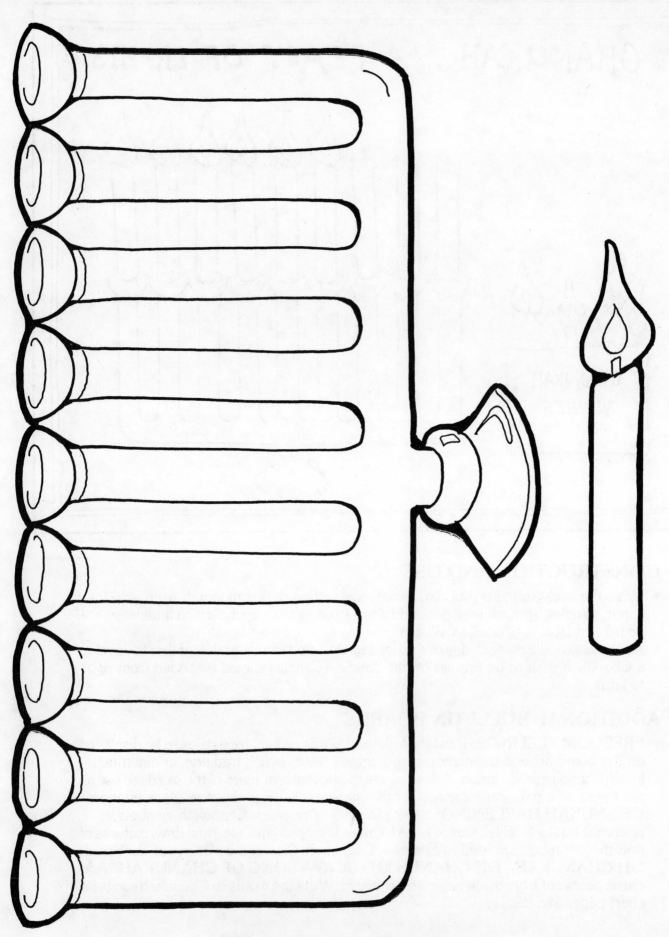

Not A Creature Was Stirring...

Except One Little Mouse

CONSTRUCTION AND USE

- Use dark blue paper for the background. Cut the mouse from gray paper, the moon (use pattern on page 9) from yellow paper and the tree and ground from black.
- Ask students to write stories or poems or draw pictures based on the bulletin board title. Display student work around the mouse. Or, make up a class story by adding a chapter a day for a week or ten days.

ADDITIONAL BULLETIN BOARDS

TWINKLE, TWINKLE LITTLE STAR: Cut stars out of yellow paper and attach to the board. Write out the words to the song Twinkle, Twinkle Little Star on a piece of paper and place beside the mouse as if he is singing.

NIGHTTIME STORIES: Write the names of several nighttime stories on a star. Display on the board. Or, display book jackets of nighttime stories.

I SAW THE MAN IN THE MOON!: Have kids write short stories about an imaginary visit with the man in the moon. Provide each child with a moon pattern and let them decorate it to use as a booklet cover for their story. Display on the board.

STARLIGHT STARBRIGHT PLEASE GRANT MY WISH TONIGHT: Have students write down a happy wish for one of their classmates. Display the wishes on the board.

Make a "star" necklace by cutting stars from heavy paper and threading them onto yarn or ribbon. The pattern may also be used to cut stencils for use in art projects.

CONSTRUCTION AND USE

● Use heavy green construction paper to make the tree. Let students design their own gift-wrap paper for the packages by following the directions below for vegetable or fruit prints.

> VEGETABLE OR FRUIT PRINTS
> ● Cut a holiday design into a piece of fruit or vegetable.
> ● Dip the design into printing ink or paint.
> ● Print the design on the packages.

● Have students decorate the tree further by making their own ornaments using the patterns provided. These can be decorated with glitter, felt tip pens, crayons, paint or other materials.

ADDITIONAL BULLETIN BOARDS

PEACE ON EARTH: Make a world peace tree by decorating the tree with ornaments cut from construction paper and labeled with peace promoting traits or actions. (Examples: sharing, courtesy, friendship, respect, honesty, etc.) The activity could be reinforced by asking students to write essays or reports on world peace.

FIND THE HIDDEN MESSAGE: Give each student a tree pattern. Tell them to decorate the tree and to include on it a secret Christmas message. Display the trees on the board and allow other students to find the hidden messages.

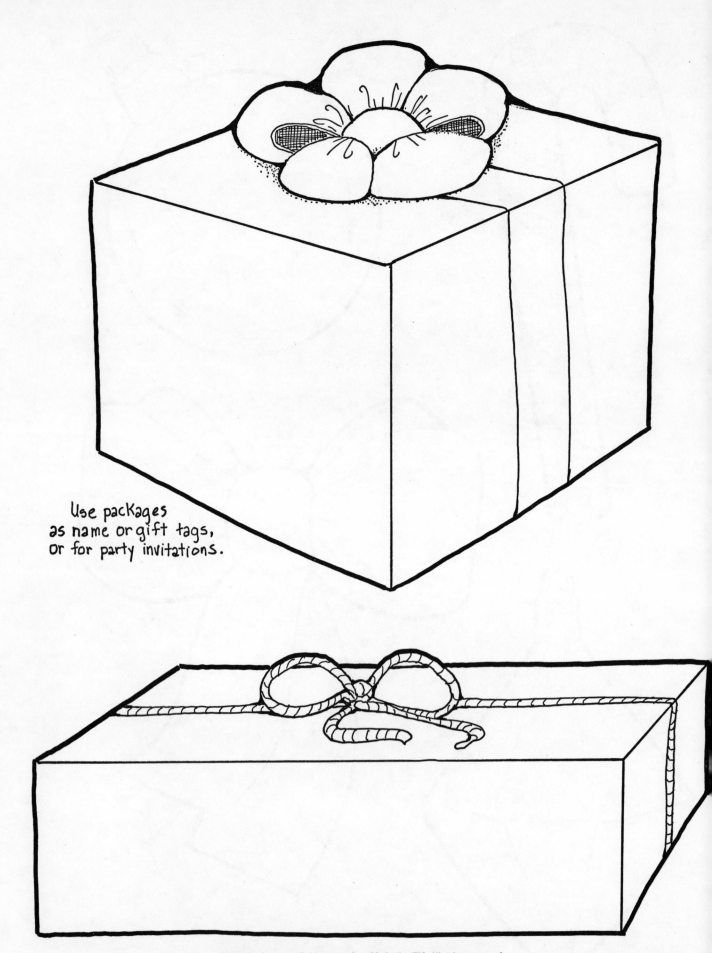

Use packages
as name or gift tags,
or for party invitations.

CONSTRUCTION AND USE

- Make the bells out of gold or silver gift-wrap paper. Use yarn, rope or ribbon for the bell pull. Make the background out of black or navy blue construction paper.
- Ask students to write New Year's resolutions around the bells. Or, give each student a small bell to write their resolutions on.

ADDITIONAL BULLETIN BOARDS

SILVER BELLS: Make the large bells from silver foil. On a piece of poster board or chart paper, write the words to the song SILVER BELLS. Enjoy singing the song with the students. (Use a record for background music if needed.) Complete the bulletin board with student illustrations.

RING IN THE NEW SCHOOL YEAR: Display a picture of each student on a small bell or, display the group picture on the big bell. Write students' names on the board. Then, let each student try to match the names and faces of their new classmates.

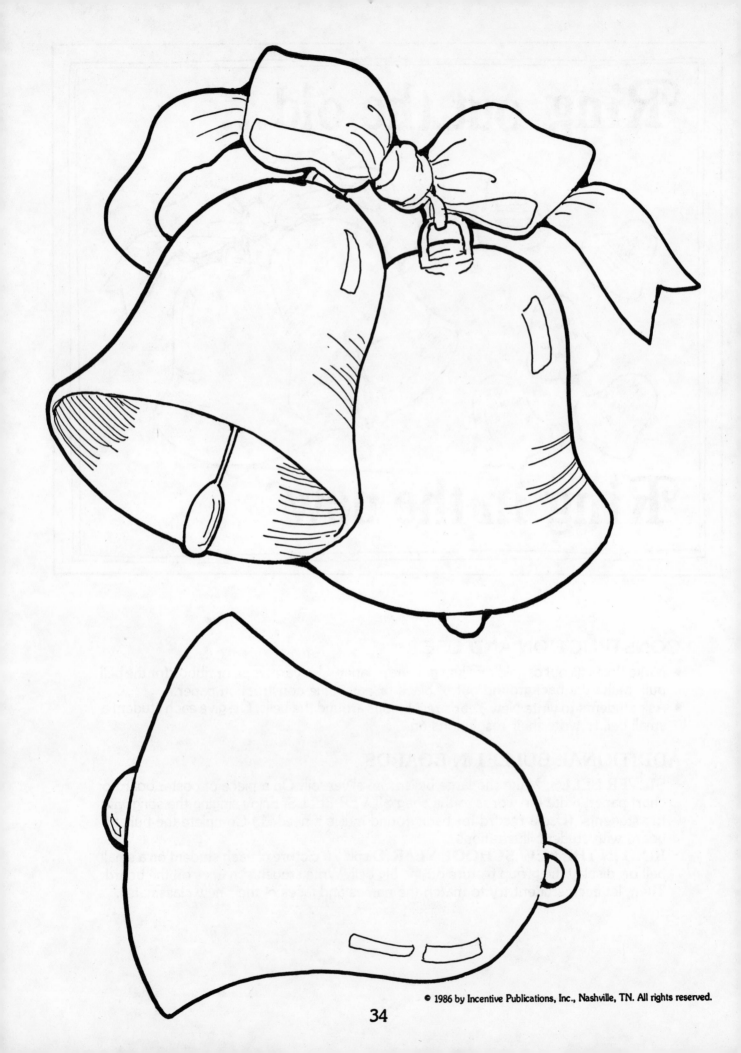

34

CONSTRUCTION AND USE

- Use light blue construction paper for the background. Make the large heart from red construction paper and attach white eyelet trim around the edges. Enlarge the cupid pattern, cut it out and color the hair yellow. Make the small hearts from red and pink.
- Provide each student with a small heart. Ask them to write on the heart something that they love. For example, I love chocolate candy, I love snowy days or I love art class. Display on the board.

ADDITIONAL BULLETIN BOARDS

OPPOSITES ATTRACT: Ask students to write antonyms in the big heart.

VALENTINE'S DAY IS A TIME TO SAY THANK-YOU: Have students make valentines for the principal, cafeteria workers, school secretary and even for the teacher. Display on the board.

SECRET VALENTINES: Have students draw names and then make a valentine for the person whose name they have drawn. Each valentine should be representative of the hobbies, interests or personality of the student whose name was drawn. Pin the valentines around the big heart with the name written on the back. Let students guess whose name is on the back.

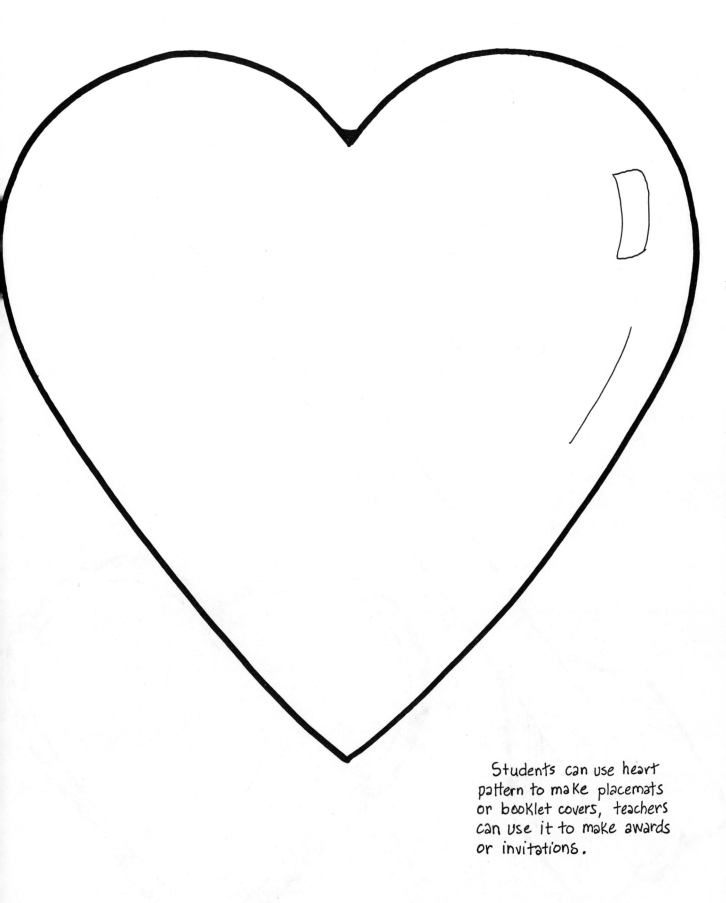

Students can use heart
pattern to make placemats
or booklet covers, teachers
can use it to make awards
or invitations.

Leaping Leprechauns!

CONSTRUCTION AND USE

- Make everything on the board from different shades of green paper.
- Have students write St. Patrick's day stories or myths to surround the leprechauns.

ADDITIONAL BULLETIN BOARDS

LEAPING LEPRECHAUNS AND OTHER MAGICAL CREATURES: Have students research and write reports on magical or mythical characters such as elves, gnomes, trolls, giants, unicorns and fairies. Display the reports on the board. Or, have students write and illustrate creative stories about mythical characters. Pin these to the board.

BE CAREFUL WHAT YOU WISH FOR . . . WISHES DO COME TRUE: Ask each student to write the one thing they most wish for on a green construction paper shamrock. Pin the wishes to the board and lead a class discussion related to what would happen if all the wishes came true.

Cut shamrocks from
green paper and use to
make "shamrock strings"
to hang from ceiling,
chalk board or window
frames.

CONSTRUCTION AND USE

● Ask students to write three words that describe the giant egg on small egg shapes. Attach the small eggs to the board around the large egg.

ADDITIONAL BULLETIN BOARDS

CAN YOU BELIEVE IT ALL STARTED WITH AN EGG?: Read "Chickens Aren't The Only Ones" written and published by Ruth Heller, 1981. Ask students to draw pictures of animals, other than chickens, that lay eggs. Cut out and pin animals around the giant egg.

EGGHEAD STORIES: Ask students to write a story, poem or play with the giant egg as the main character. Reproduce the egg pattern as a booklet cover. Display the stories on the board.

EGG-STRA SPECIAL EASTER WISHES: Ask each student to make an egg from pastel colored construction paper and write a wish for someone special on the egg. On the last day of school before Easter, eggs can be removed from the board to be presented as Easter cards.

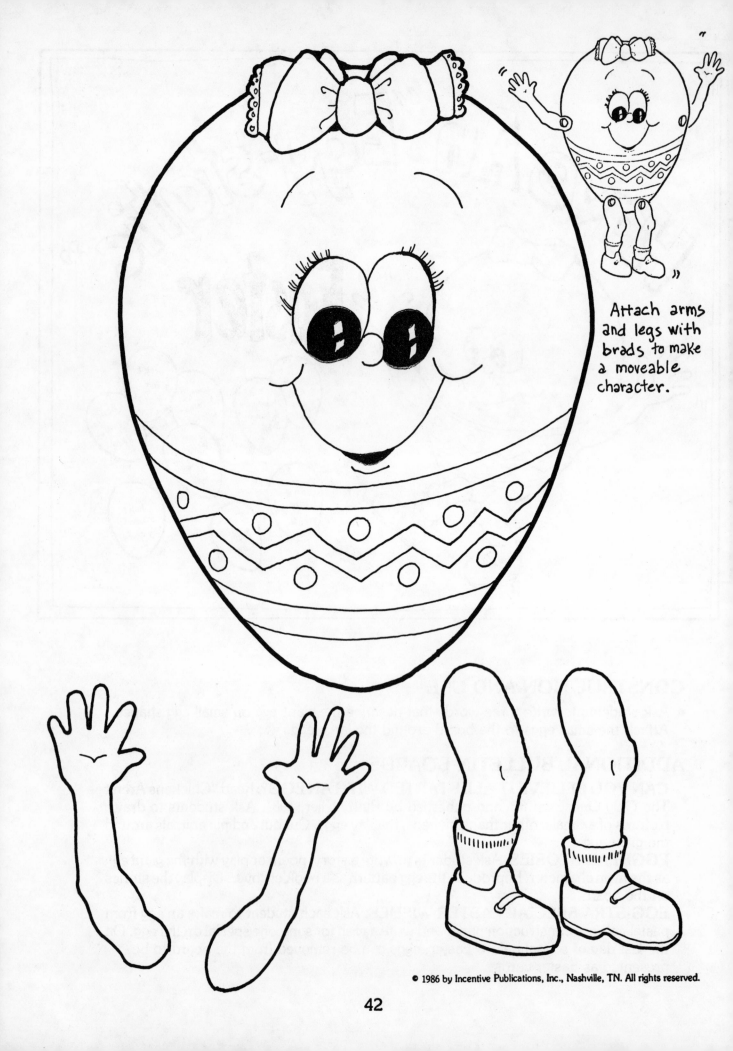

Attach arms
and legs with
brads to make
a moveable
character.

A Tisket, A Tasket, Fill The Easter Basket !

CONSTRUCTION AND USE

- Enlarge the basket pattern and cut it out of brightly colored construction paper. Make the background blue, the grass green and the rabbit white.
- Cut eggs from different colors of construction paper. Ask each student to take an egg, cut it into two pieces in a zigzag pattern and use to make a word or math puzzle. For math puzzles, the problems may be written on one piece of the puzzle and the answer on the other. Use the same concept with word puzzles using abbreviations, compound words or words and meanings. Put all puzzle pieces in a box near the board. During free time, students may go to the board and try to match egg halves. Both pieces of the matched egg may then be pinned inside the basket. The object of the activity is to "fill the basket" each day.

ADDITIONAL BULLETIN BOARDS

HAVE YOU READ THESE?: Fill the basket with book jackets.

VOCABULARY TREATS: Ask students to draw and cut out treats (chocolate bunnies, jelly beans, eggs or chicks). Then have them print a new vocabulary word on the front of the treat and display in the basket.

HAPPY EASTER FROM THE TEACHER: A special treat from the teacher can be printed on the back of each egg to be enjoyed at a specified time each day. (Example: free reading time, extra playtime, read aloud time, etc.)

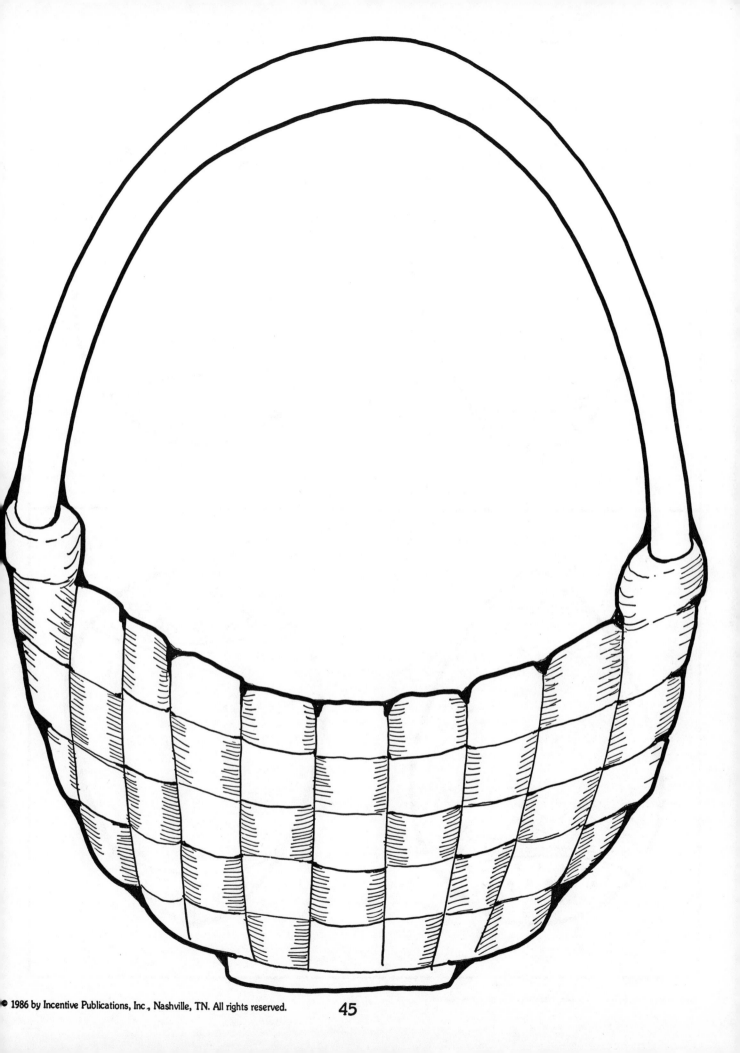

Cut along dotted lines and have students color the eggs to make Easter cards.

CONSTRUCTION AND USE

- Cut the clown from any large sheet of paper available. Make ruffles, hat, shoes, buttons and facial features from contrasting colors of construction paper (the brighter the better).
- Cut large letters for the caption from bright yellow, blue or magenta paper and use felt tip pens to add designs or "doodles" to capture student interest.
- Display special student work on the board.

ADDITIONAL BULLETIN BOARDS

JUST CLOWNING AROUND: Cut a second clown (see pattern) from complementary colors and add to the board. Ask students to write jokes and riddles for display on the board.

APRIL FOOL'S DAY FOOLERS: Ask students to draw crazy, mixed up April Fool's day pictures to display on the board.

THE CIRCUS IS COMING TO TOWN: Use the clown as a part of a circus theme board. Ask students to draw pictures of various circus activities to display on the board.

MATH UNDER THE BIG TOP: Cut balloons from various colors of paper. Print multiplication, addition, subtraction or division facts on the balloons. Use the board for skill reinforcement.

48

Use clown patterns to make stand-up decorations, booklet covers and paper bag puppets.

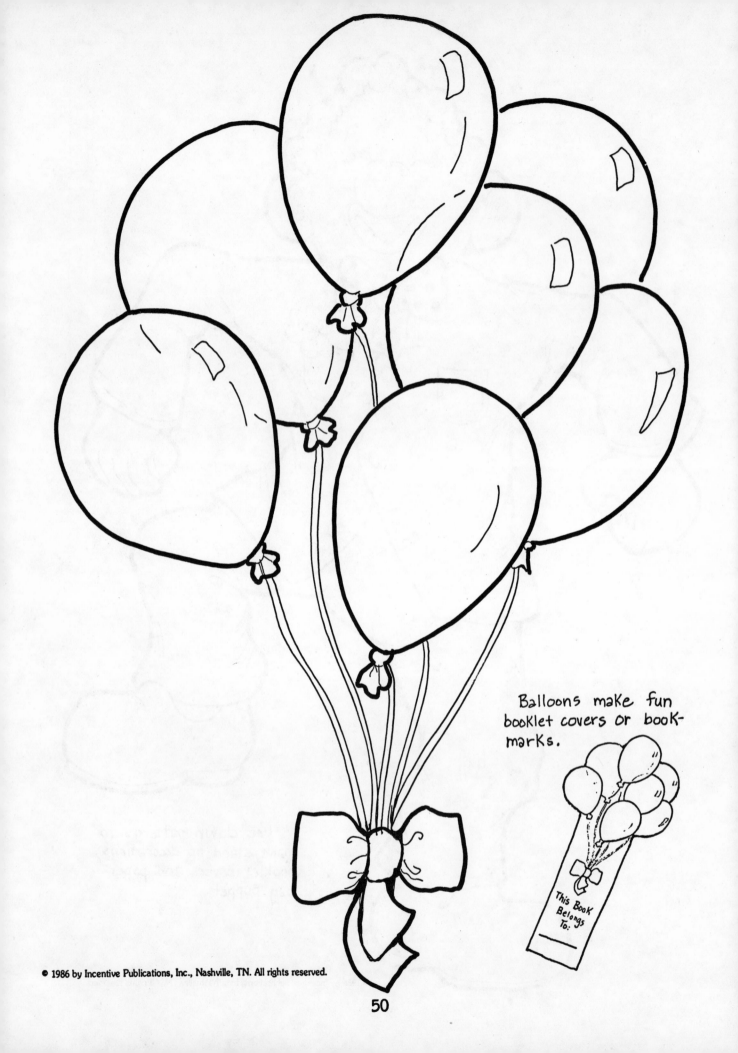

Balloons make fun
booklet covers or book-
marks.

CONSTRUCTION AND USE

- Make the Maypole from brown construction paper. Use pastel colored crepe paper, wide ribbon or construction paper for the streamers.
- Ask students to cut free-form flowers, birds and bees (or use the patterns on pages 52, 55, 56) to carry out the May Day theme. Display the artwork around the Maypole.

ADDITIONAL BULLETIN BOARDS

RING AROUND THE WORLD: Ask students to draw and cut out children (or use boy and girl pattern on page 52) dressed in costumes worn in countries around the world. Label the country or origin and display the cutouts around the Maypole.
RING AROUND THE MAYPOLE WITH GOOD WORK (GOOD STUDY HABITS, KINDNESS AND COURTESY or GOOD HEALTH HABITS): Display appropriate student work around the Maypole.
DANCE INTO SPRING WITH POETRY: Ask students to write original poetry with spring themes or copy and illustrate favorite poems from anthologies to display around the Maypole.

Use flowers to fill Easter basket (pg.43), or to make a necklace, lei, or headband.

CONSTRUCTION AND USE

- Make the background sky from blue construction paper, the grass from green paper and the sun from yellow. Enlarge the pool pattern and have students color it in with markers or paints.
- Display book jackets for summer reading around the pool.

ADDITIONAL BULLETIN BOARDS

SPLASH INTO ART: Surround the pool with student artwork.

SPLASH INTO MATH: Surround the pool with math flash cards or homework papers.

SPLASH INTO A SUPER SUMMER - LEARN SOMETHING NEW!: Have students write down something new that they plan to learn during the summer. Display on the board.

THE BIRDS AND BEES KNOW, SPRING IS HERE!: Use flowers, birds, bees and rainbows to form a background for student reports on spring weather and weather related subjects. Display the daily weather report on the board. It might be fun to make a class weather prediction on the day before and compare it with the actual report.

Use as a "happy face" or
"Sunshine Award."

Use birds as finger or stick
puppets ; use nest and birds
in science or seasonal activities.

FALL BORDER PATTERNS

FOLD

FOLD

Use for board on page 47.

FOLD

FOLD

FOLD

FOLD

Use for board on page 13.

FOLD

FOLD

Use for boards on pages 7 or 13.

FOLD

FOLD

FOLD

Use for boards on pages 7, 13 or 19.

FOLD

FOLD

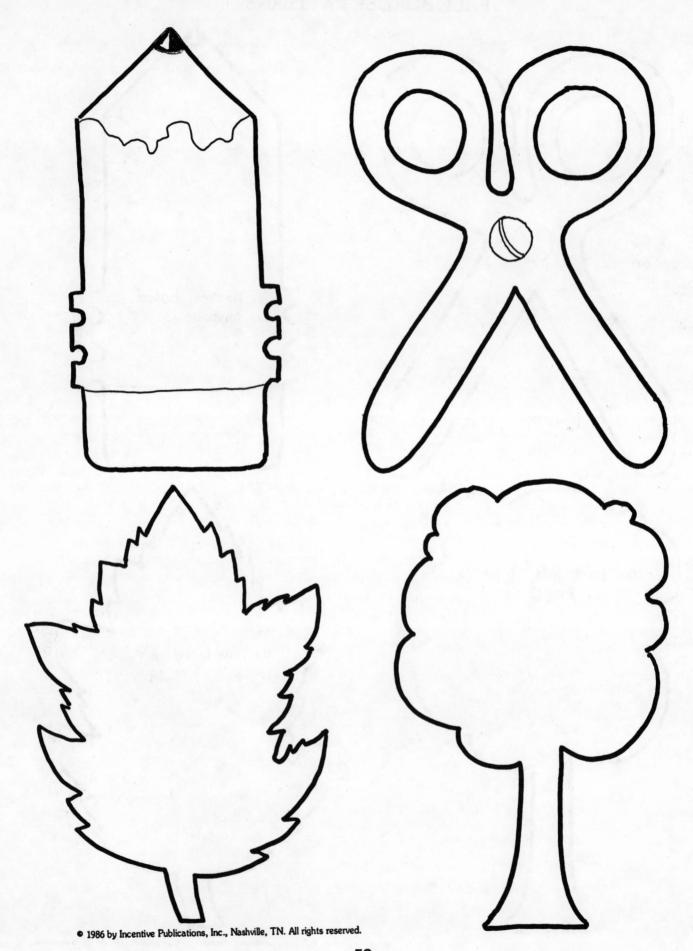

WINTER BORDER PATTERNS

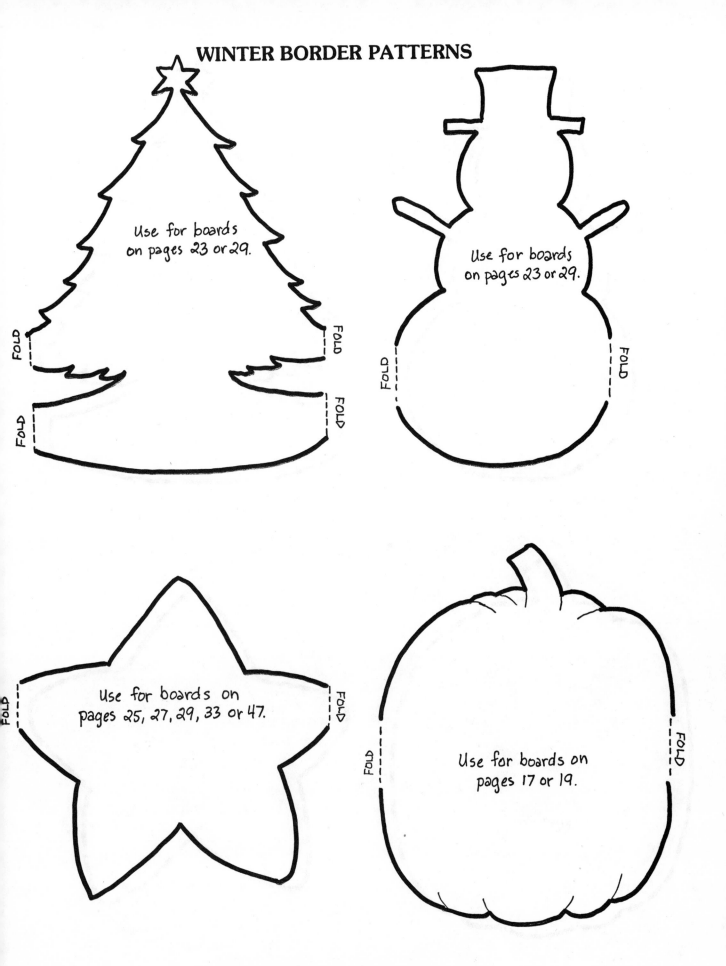

Use for boards on pages 23 or 29.

Use for boards on pages 23 or 29.

Use for boards on pages 25, 27, 29, 33 or 47.

Use for boards on pages 17 or 19.

SPRING BORDER PATTERNS

FOLD

Use for boards on pages 39, 43 or 51.

FOLD

FOLD

Use for boards on pages 41, 43 or 51.

FOLD

FOLD

FOLD

Use for boards on pages 41, 43 or 51.

FOLD

FOLD

Use for boards on pages 41 or 43.

FOLD

MISCELLANEOUS BORDER PATTERNS

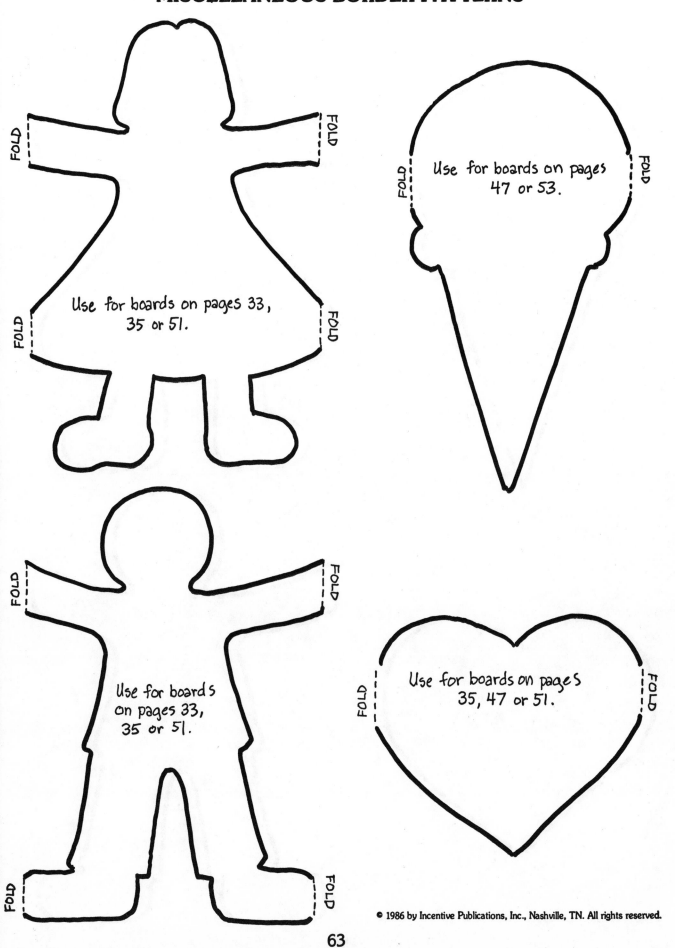

FOLD

FOLD

Use for boards on pages 47 or 53.

FOLD

FOLD

FOLD

FOLD

Use for boards on pages 33, 35 or 51.

FOLD

FOLD

FOLD

FOLD

Use for boards on pages 33, 35 or 51.

FOLD

FOLD

Use for boards on pages 35, 47 or 51.

FOLD

FOLD